Extreme Dot-to-Dot Beautiful Birds
Puzzles from 385 to 797 Dots

By Dottie's Crazy Dot-to-Dots

Copyright © 2017 by Lilt House

All rights reserved. This book or any portion thereof
may not be reproduced or used in any manner whatsoever
without the express written permission of the publisher
except for the use of brief quotations in a book review.

WELCOME!

Dot to dot books for adults are relaxing and fun.
The directions are simple: Find dot #1,
and draw a line from that dot to dot #2,
and continue on. As you connect the dots,
the picture will take shape.

Take your time and don't stress,
there is always another dot,
and you will always find it.

This book contains 20 beautiful images for you
and 4 bonus images from other dot to dot book.
We've also included a link to a pdf online where you
can download and print the images from this book,
in case you wish to connect the dots again!
You'll find that in the last pages of this book.

Find a mistake in one of our books?
Email us and tell us about it
and get a free dot to dot book!
Email: LiltKidsColoring@gmail.com
We hope you enjoy this dot to dot book!

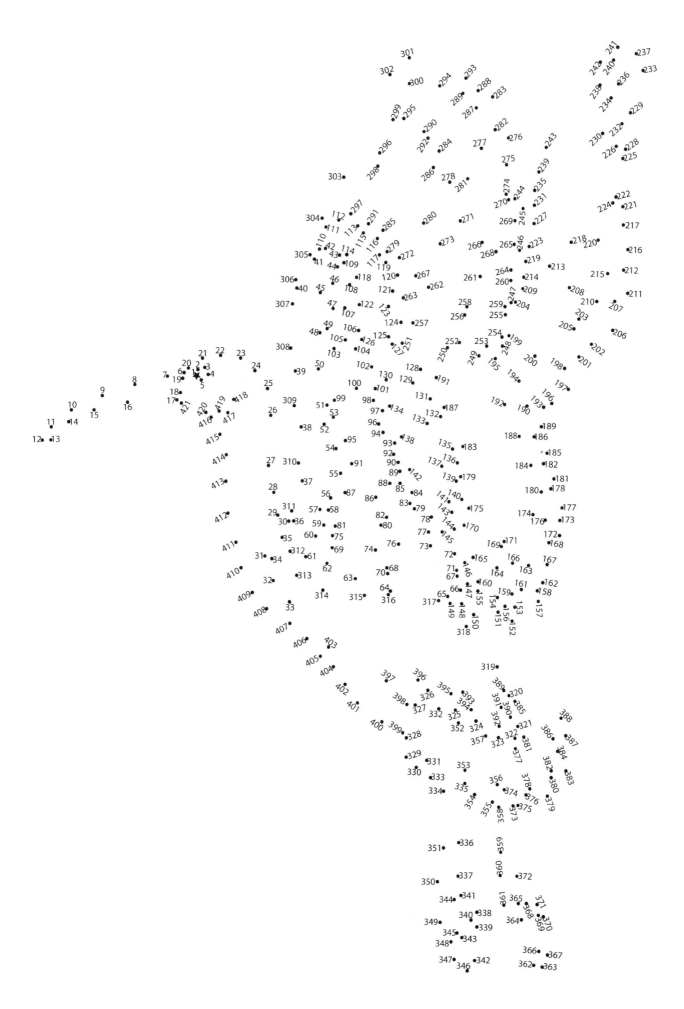

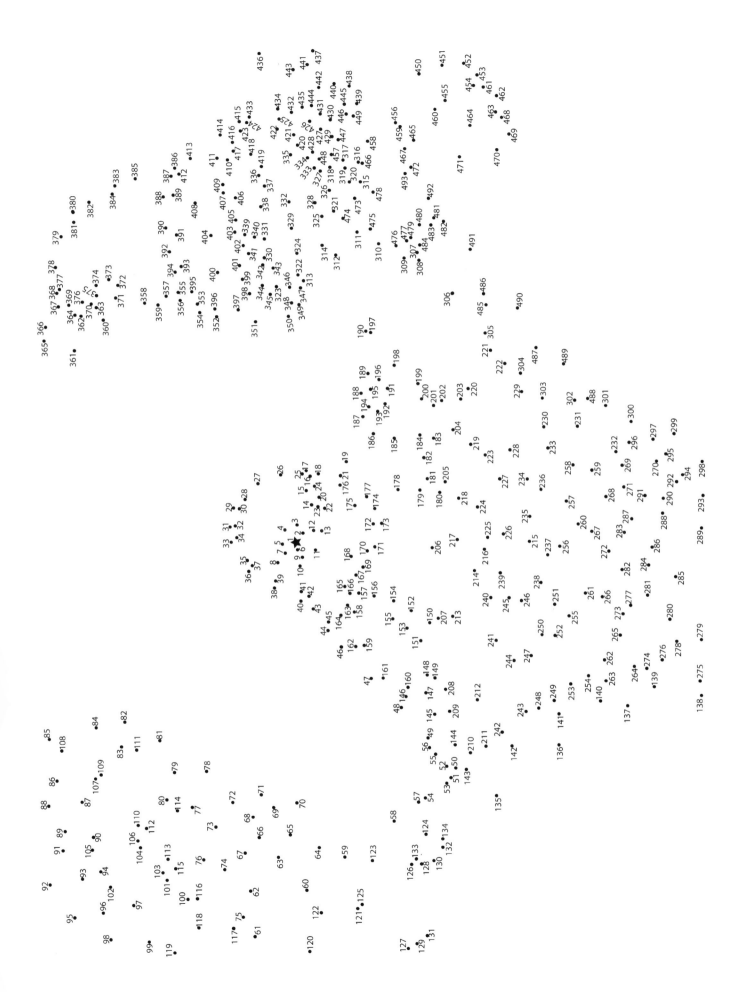

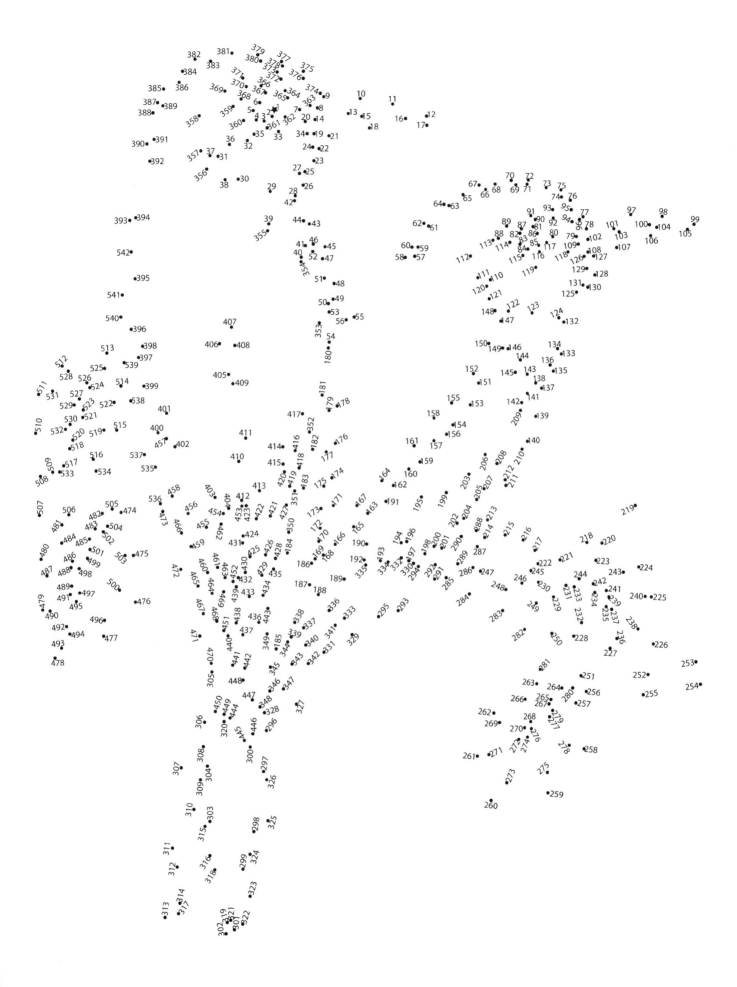

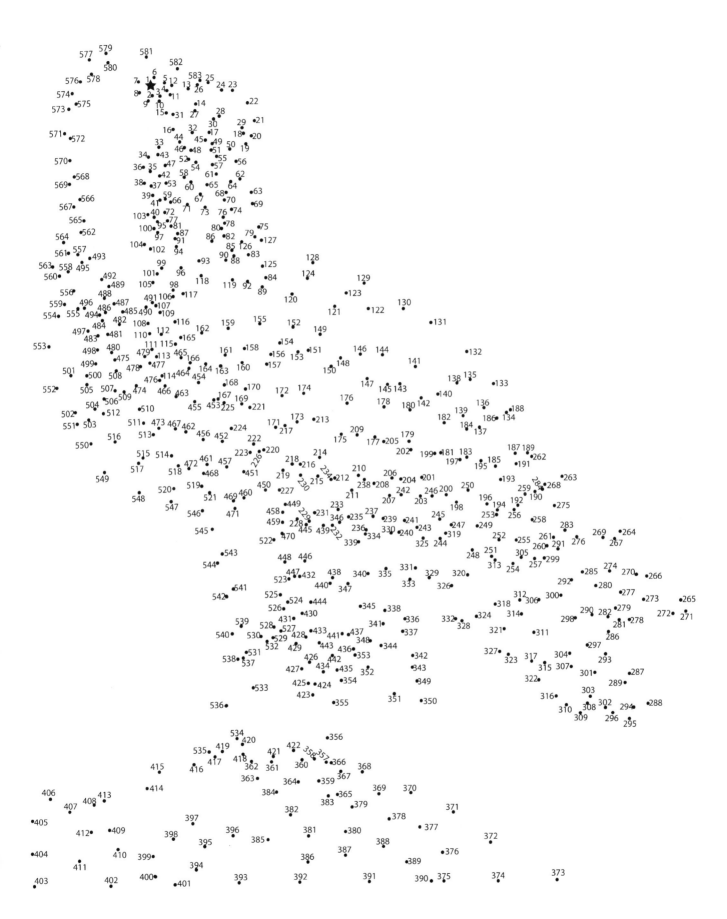

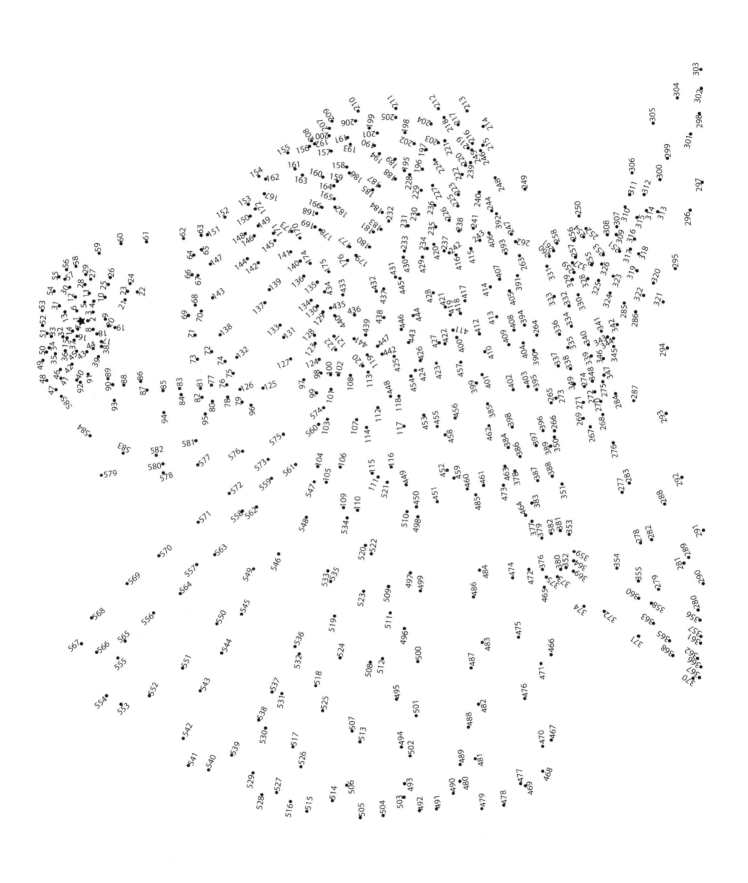

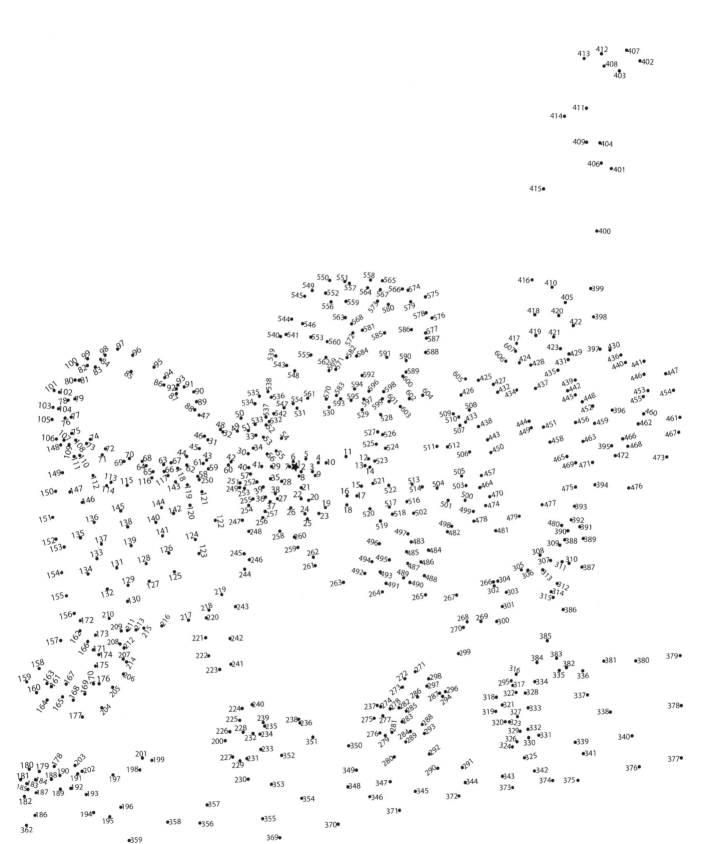

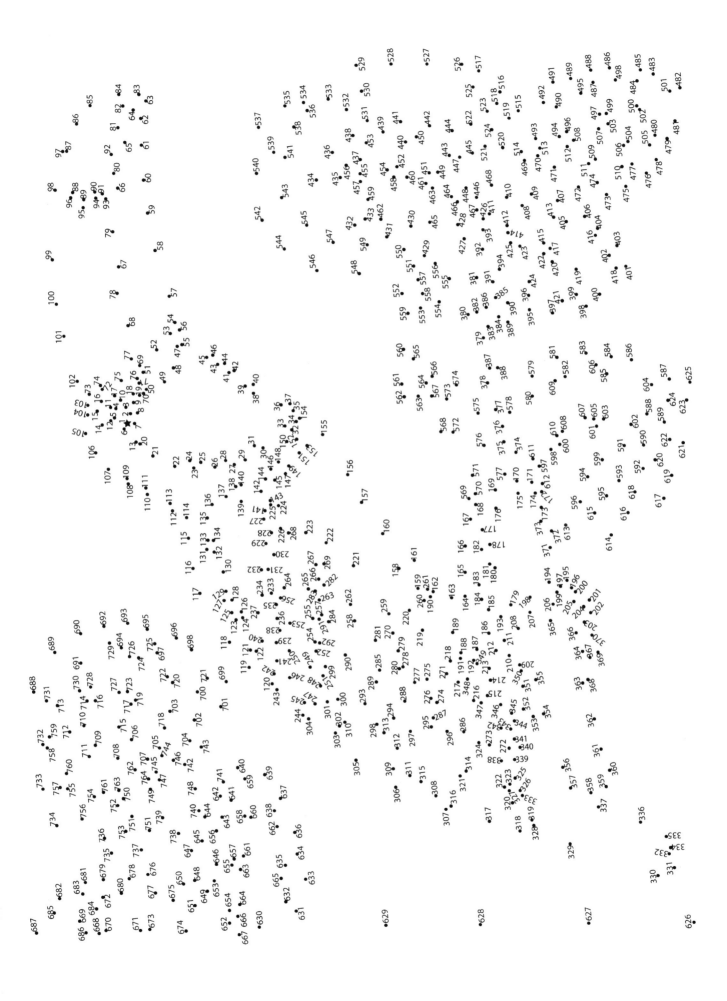

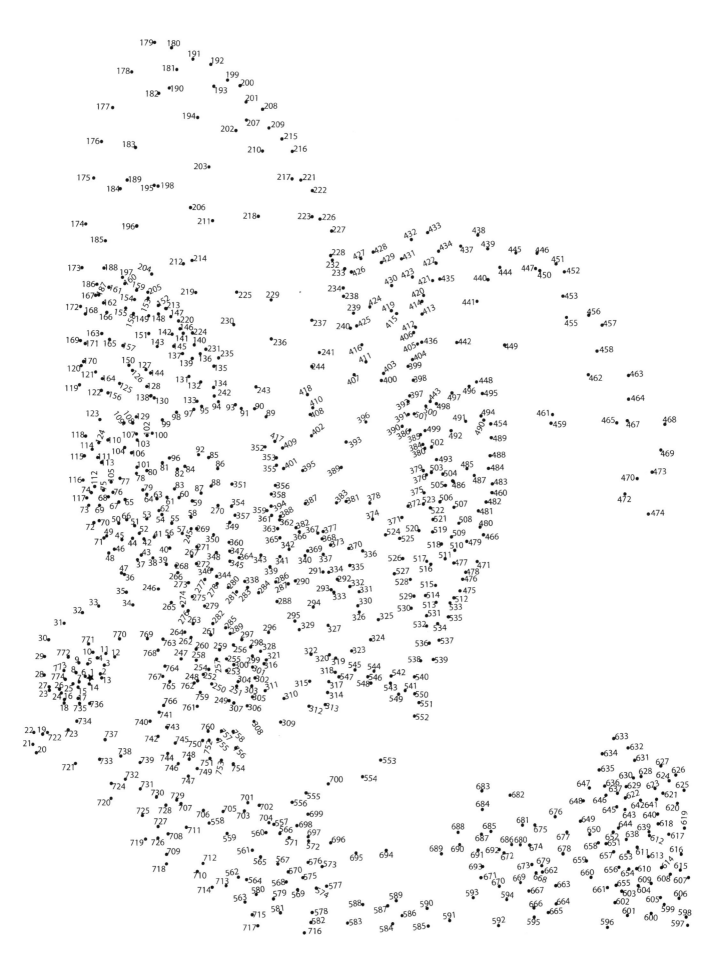

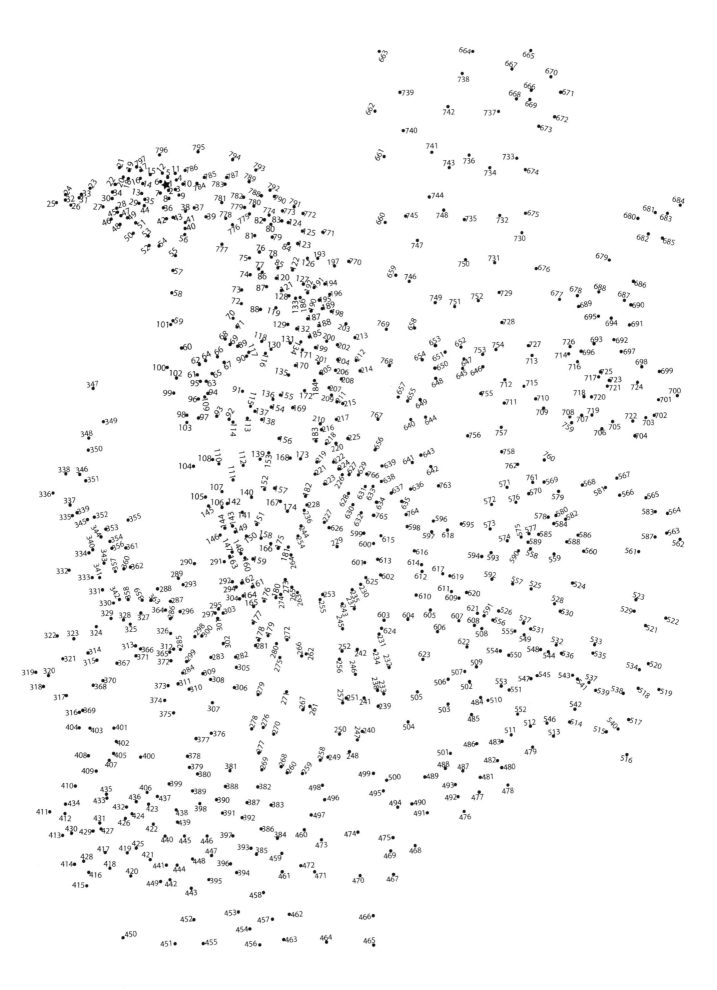

Enjoy a couple of bonus images from our other Dot-to-Dot Books

Find our books on Amazon.

Big Book of Dot-to-Dot Animals:
Stress Relieving and Relaxing Puzzles

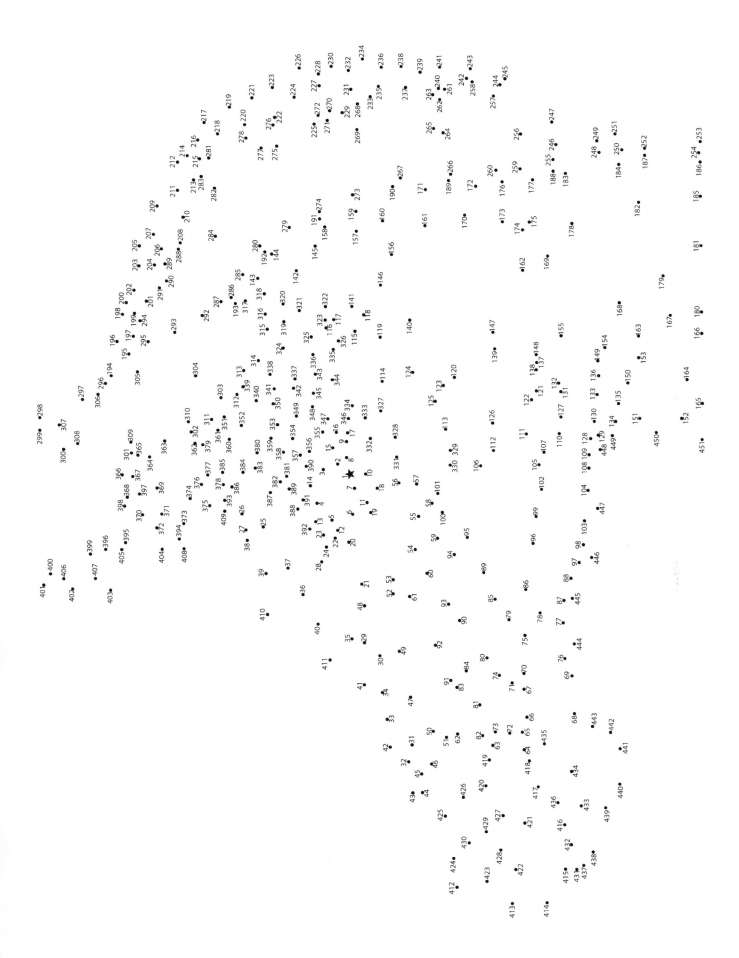

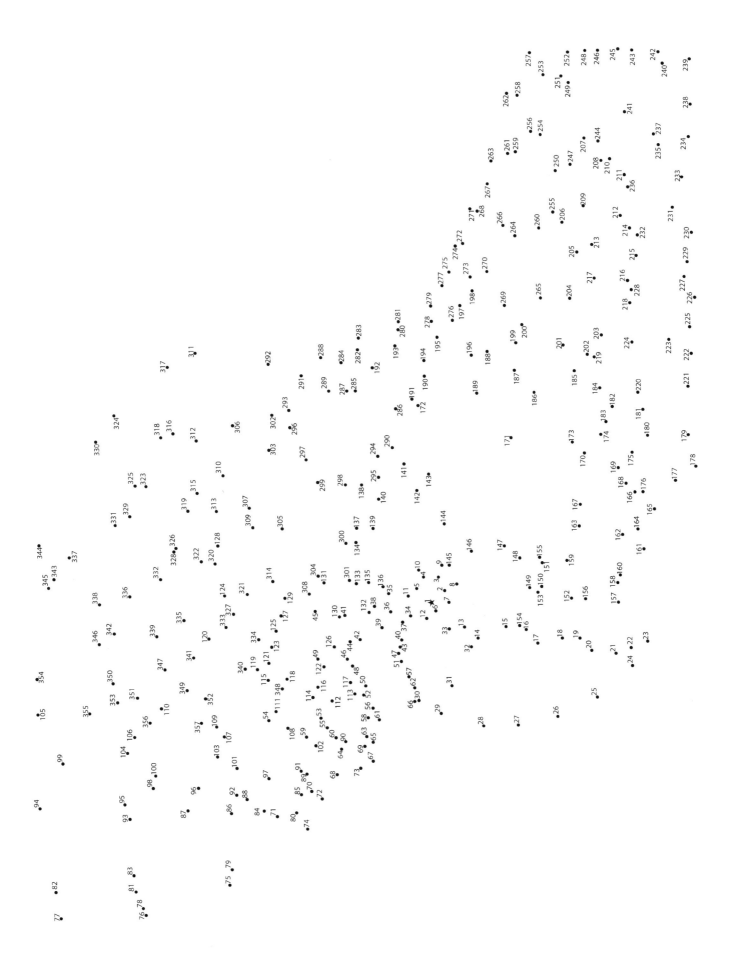

Easy to Read Dot-to-Dots
Large Print Puzzles from 303-563 Dots

This Dot to Dot book comes with a free printable PDF version - so you can print another one when you are done with this one!

Go to

Liltkids.com/dot-to-dot-42610

to download it.

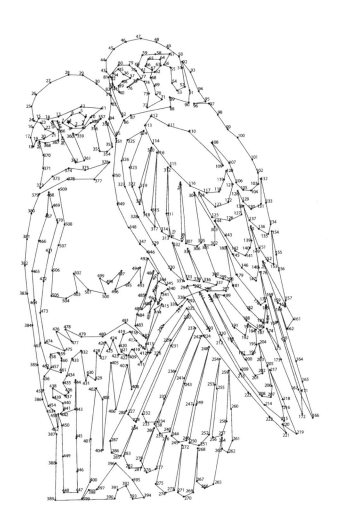

Answer Key

(start from top left to right)

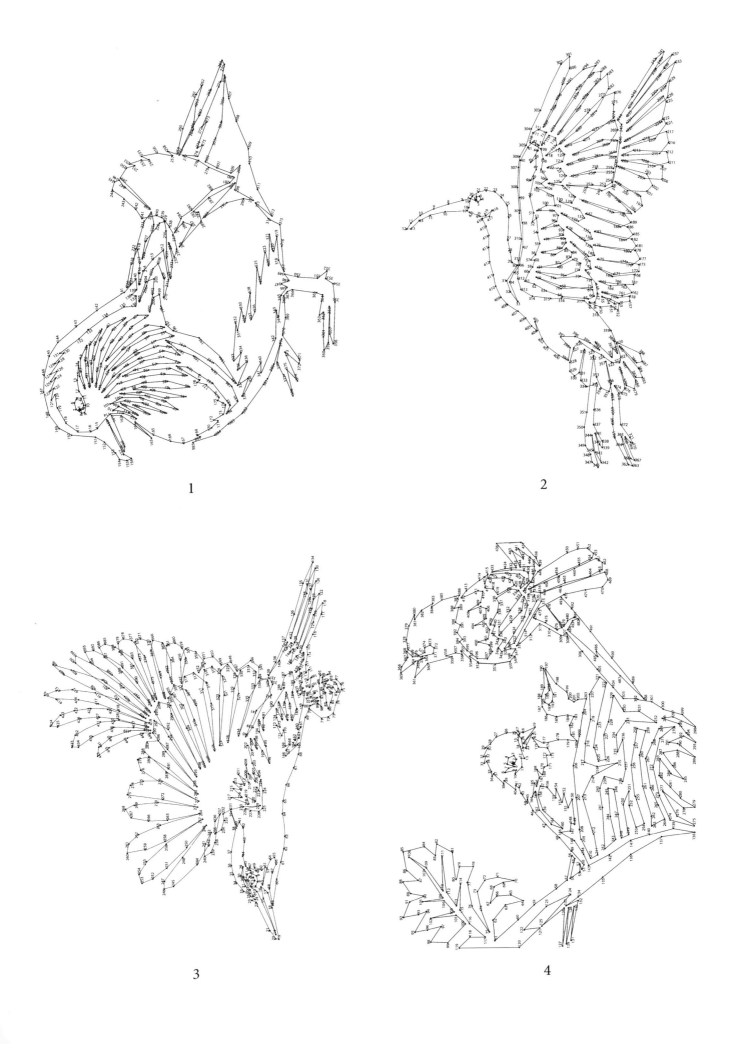

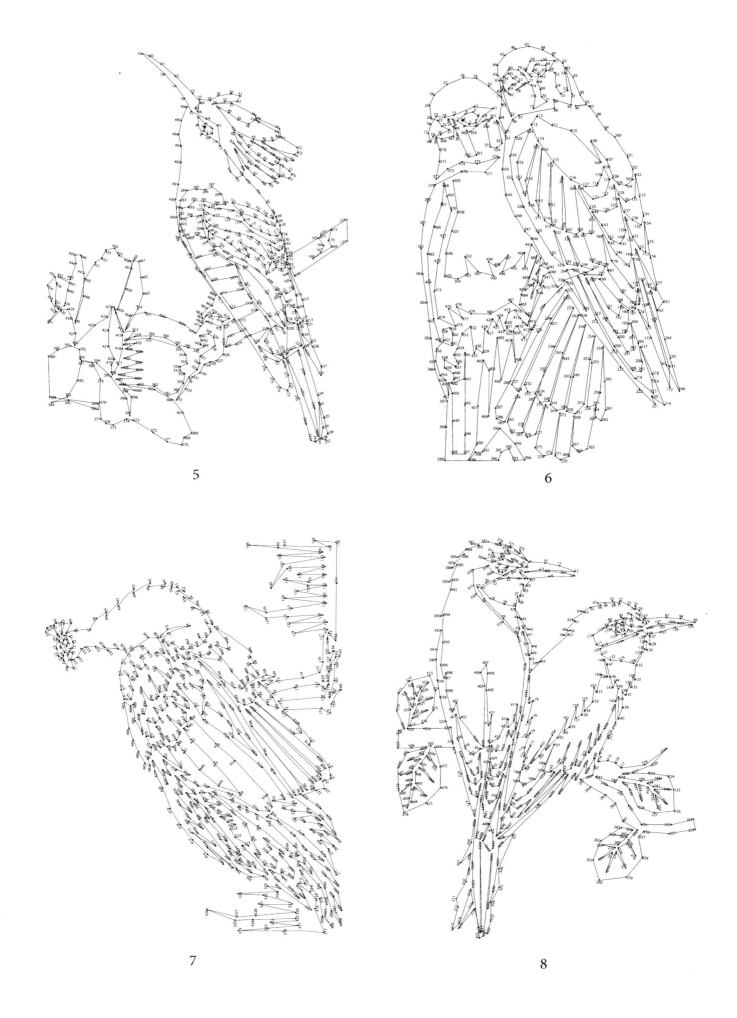

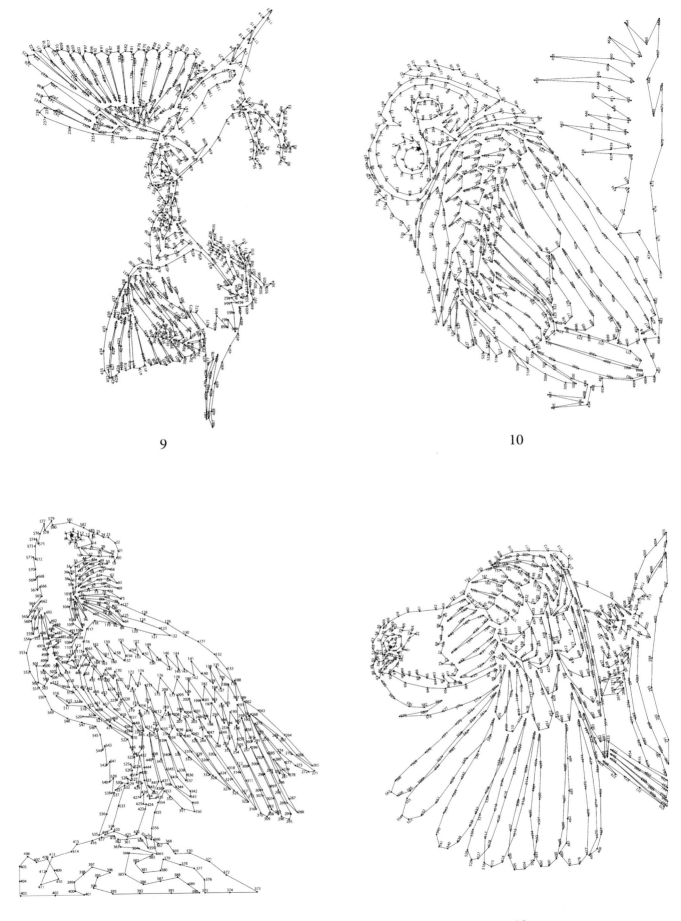

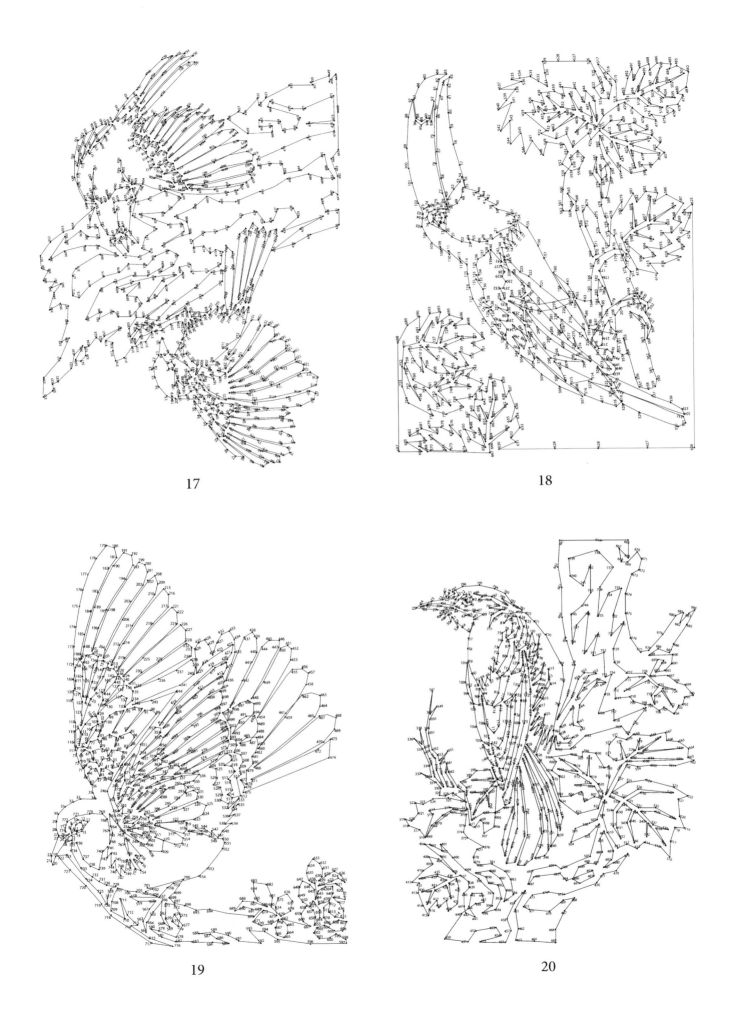

Made in the USA
Lexington, KY
27 September 2017